BORN IN THE 50s

BORN IN THE 50s

TIM GLYNNE-JONES

ARCTURUS

ARCTURUS

This edition published in 2021 by
Arcturus Publishing Limited
26/27 Bickels Yard, 151–153 Bermondsey Street,
London SE1 3HA

Copyright © Arcturus Holdings Limited

ISBN: 978-1-78212-885-4
AD003959UK

Printed in China

Contents

Introduction

The Fifties was a decade in which Britain put its house in order. While the Forties had been played out against a backdrop of war, the Fifties had an altogether calmer air about them. The old standards of politeness and respectability still held firm, but people were discovering new freedoms in terms of transport, labour, style and self-expression. This book depicts the cultural shifts that made the Fifties such a defining era in British history in a collection of fascinating pictures and written recollections that bring back those halcyon days, in which innocence and impudence walked hand in hand.

Like steam released from a pressure cooker, the Fifties saw Britain expanding at a rate of knots, and as a consequence gaps opened up in its once tight-knit society: gaps between classes, gaps between sexes, gaps between races, gaps between generations. War was not entirely off the agenda. There was Suez and Korea, not to mention the Cold War and the looming fear of the hydrogen bomb. There was conflict within society too. The Fifties saw race riots and gang fights, infrequent yet stark reminders that everything in the garden was not quite as rosy as the Prime Minister Harold Macmillan would have everyone believe.

The Empire was dwindling too, for better or worse, no-one was entirely sure, yet there was much for Britons to celebrate: they had a new queen, they conquered Everest, broke the four-minute mile and produced some of the world's best motor cars.

Every patriotic headline and each great innovation touched the people more quickly and compellingly than ever before, via the mushrooming new medium of television.

America was becoming a growing influence in the Fifties; its films, its music, its literature, its fashions and its technologies would all play a major part in changing the British way of life. It was the era of Elvis Presley, Bill Haley and Buddy Holly, of James Dean and Marilyn Monroe, Jack Kerouac and J.D. Salinger. These groundbreaking influences tapped into the suppressed emotions of British adolescents, giving them the confidence and inspiration to break free from the conventional expectations of family life – a life still trussed up with Victorian values – and go in search of their own fulfilment. The English language acquired a new word: teenager.

For mum and dad, the demands of teenage children were an unwelcome nuisance. Convenience was key: cars, supermarkets, washing machines and vacuum cleaners were all coming within reach of more and more people and the more they got, the more they wanted. Holidays too had a brighter look about them. This was the golden age of the holiday camp, Butlin's and Pontins, chalets for the family, communal dances and talent contests.

By the end of the decade, Britain had become a vastly different place from the country that had crawled blinking out of the Forties: cleaner, faster, younger and more exciting. It had plastic and jet planes, rock'n'roll and fish fingers. Perhaps Macmillan was right: most people had never had it so good.

A child carrying a cache of fireworks receives a gentle word of warning from a local bobby. The Fifties saw the boom of a generation that had never known war – an untainted, hopeful generation that was enjoying new freedoms such as the end of sweet rationing, and found it hard to understand the social

Young Scamps

and moral constraints to which their parents still adhered. The idea that children should be seen and not heard still prevailed throughout much of society and, to begin with, few children dared to buck the trend. After a decade of brutal reality, there appeared to be a concerted effort on the part of adult society to re-establish childish innocence through strict discipline, and they had a new weapon in their armoury: television. As the black-and-white 'box' became more and more prevalent in ordinary homes, there was precious little coming from the single BBC channel to incite the young generation to rebel. That part would be played by the new role models from American cinema and music, such as James Dean and Elvis Presley.

With a look of bemusement, four young children watch the antics of Andy Pandy on the 'box'. The television puppet, who made his debut in the summer of 1950, set the trend for children's television entertainment and its memorable theme tunes for decades to come.

Two young pioneers discover the advantages of running upright as a group of four-year-olds compete in a summer sports day, watched by an eager crowd of proud parents. In the Fifties it was quite acceptable for young children to give full rein to their competitive instincts.

After the lean war years, cakes were much prized in the Fifties. Here, our young party host finds he can't keep up with demand as tolerance looks to be wearing thin on the faces of those queuing for a slice. 'I could do a much better job than that,' they're all thinking.

*A train driver smiles down on children in their nine-seater
pram at smoke-filled Euston Station. The Peter Rabbit
Hotel was advertised in the Lytham St Annes Express
as 'a small first class hotel for children only'. Babies were
charged 1.5 guineas a week, and over-2s a guinea.*

Boy power

• •

Two friends enjoy the luxury of private motor travel, propelled by a third boy with a strong pair of legs. Although these boys appear to have the street to themselves, real cars were rapidly taking over and soon such boyish games would have to be confined to the pavement. Or perhaps the race track, for this was a time of renaissance for motor racing. The first Formula One Grand Prix took place at Silverstone in 1950 and, throughout the decade, boys marvelled at the driving feats of Juan Manuel Fangio, Stirling Moss and Giuseppe Farina.

This is a particularly impressive example of the motorless car, or go-cart as it came to be known. In most cases it comprised little more than a few bits of wood, maybe a crate to sit on, a set of pram wheels, a length of rope for steering and, for the safety conscious, some form of brake, usually a block of wood which rubbed on one wheel, causing the whole contraption to veer violently across the road.

Left *A boy stands on a chair to look in a stamp seller's window. Philately enjoyed a boom in popularity in the Fifties as the face of Queen Elizabeth II replaced her father on Britain's stamps, and any boy with a Penny Red in his possession achieved legendary status amongst his peers.*

Right *A young girl seeks to emulate the great movie directors of the time – such as John Huston or Alfred Hitchcock – with one of the new cine cameras that were becoming increasingly fashionable for capturing family occasions on celluloid. The people were discovering home movies.*

FLOWER POWER *Two children walk hand in hand through London's Covent Garden clutching bunches of flowers. Covent Garden was still a renowned flower market in the Fifties and in 1954 it celebrated its 300th year as a fruit and vegetable market. But its days as a market place were numbered.*

Down by the riverside

Three children amuse themselves on the steps by the River Thames at Custom House in the Royal Victoria Dock. The lighter pulling away from the quayside and the mass of cranes across the water are evidence of a dockland at the height of its powers, at the time the largest commercial port in the world, taking in exotic goods from throughout the empire and sending forth the produce of Britain's thriving manufacturing industries. At their peak London's docklands comprised seven enclosed docks, covering 720 acres in total, with a combined 35 miles of quayside. For kids who liked boats, it was a hive of constant activity and a place to see some of the biggest ships in the world. For local residents, you could look along your street and see a ship taking up the whole of one end. But the Fifties turned out to be the swansong for London's docklands. Having been heavily bombed during the war, they were extensively repaired and enjoyed a revival in fortunes right through to the 1960s, when the advent of big containers and bigger ships rendered them sadly inadequate.

KNEES TOGETHER

Five young girls look on attentively as their headmistress demonstrates the correct deportment when riding a bicycle (or tricycle in this case): straight back, ankles tucked in, hat cocked slightly to one side. Posture and deportment were important lessons to learn for girls wishing to go anywhere in life.

Party for the world

Swiss roll, fruitcake and Coca-Cola are on the menu
at a Christmas party for children from diverse ethnic
backgrounds at one of the new comprehensive schools in
London. In need of a labour force to rebuild the country
in the wake of the war, Britain had introduced a so-called
'open-door policy' that made it easy for immigrants to come
and find work. Initially the majority were from Europe, mainly
Poland, with significant communities of Irish and Italians also
growing in England's big cities. But the Fifties saw a major
rise in immigrants from the Commonwealth, particularly the
West Indies and the recently independent and partitioned
Indian subcontinent: India, Pakistan, Bangladesh. From a
population numbering in the low thousands, these ethnic
groups quickly grew towards the millions during the decade,
later forcing Britain as a whole to recognize itself as a
multi-cultural society. The transition was not without its
difficulties, but the cultural contribution of this new wave of
new British, in terms of food and music in particular, would
become key features in the landscape of British life.

Left *Don't say lean back! A young girl looks less than happy about finding herself perched atop a half-ton boar called Purdon King Alfred 7th. Visits to the countryside often ended up with some kind of brush with the livestock at the hands of a jolly herdsman looking to liven up his day.*

Right *A boy plays dead in the road, probably not the best place to play dead. The war years had not dampened parents' enthusiasm for letting their sons play with toy guns and games like cowboys and Indians, cops and robbers and war were enough to keep boys occupied for hours.*

For children growing up in the Fifties, friends were the
secret to happiness. The only regular source of laid-on
entertainment was the Saturday Morning Pictures; television
was still for the minority and children's programmes were

You Need Friends

few and far between,
computers were for
atomic scientists and
the Premium Bond draw, and music came mostly via your
parents' radio, so most of the time you relied on your
friends as your source of entertainment. There were strict
standards of behaviour expected of children but they were
also given a lot of freedom by comparison with today's lot.
Parents were more confident about letting their children
go off on their own, without fear of them getting run over
by cars or being abducted by strangers. Consequently, the
best adventures that children of the Fifties recall rarely
feature any adults at all, let alone parents. Friends looked
after one another, challenged one another and inspired one
another. They stimulated each other's imaginations and the
games flowed as a result. On the flipside, to find yourself
without friends, or kept away from them as a punishment,
was the ultimate in misery.

Left *Two very smartly dressed schoolboys look somewhat self-conscious about having to pose with their arms round one another. This sort of physical contact between friends was not the norm in the Fifties and these two are just about young enough to get away with it.*

Above *A young girl enjoys the company of a chimpanzee at London Zoo as they while away an afternoon with a game of chess. One of the highlights of a visit to the zoo was the chimps' tea party, a daily ritual which inspired a series of adverts for PG Tips tea that began in 1956.*

DON'T TOUCH THE ROLLER! *A group of children play chase in the salubrious surrounds of a London mews while the garagemen keep a protective watch over their vehicles. As there are boys and girls involved, it's probably a game of kiss chase, a fine pastime that sharpened your running speed and gave girls an exhilarating sense of power.*

Still to discover the joys of 24-hour television, children entertained themselves with outdoor games like leapfrog. One boy assumes the textbook 'frog' position while the others take it in turns to leap over him. Good, clean, physical fun that could keep children occupied for hours on end.

Five friends from London peer through the railings at a show provided as part of the Holidays at Home week. This scheme was designed for children around Britain whose families couldn't afford to go away on summer holidays, engaging them in games and entertainments to give them a taste of the holiday spirit.

Two boys take different approaches to the old problem of meeting your enemy round a tight corner. Throughout the Fifties there was no shortage of war films from which to draw their inspiration, though the guns themselves were more likely replicas from the Wild West.

Four boys stand nervously waiting to find out which of them has been designated groom as a young make-believe bride picks her way over the rubble of a Liverpool slum to the altar. Not quite the wedding scenario she'd dreamed of, perhaps, but a lovely day for it nonetheless.

KNEES-UP *Two girls from London's East End celebrate the Coronation in 1953 with a dance in the street. Dancing was still very much a two-person affair, with most children learning some formal dance steps to take into adulthood, whether it be ballroom, swing, jive or jitterbug.*

Spellbound

Saturday Morning Pictures remained a cornerstone of the
entertainment world for children growing up in the Fifties.
For many of them it was the highlight of the week, a festival
of sweets and moving pictures on a screen with sound –
still something of a novelty at that time – all for just a few
pennies. First came the queue, then the crush, then seats
and a singsong, orchestrated by a compere and an organist
who rose up out of the stage. The words were projected
on the screen and the children sang along with gusto.
Sometimes there were games and competitions. And then
came the movies themselves, an assortment of cartoons
and funny shorts, followed by a feature or two, ending with
a cliffhanger to make sure you came back next week. When
it was all over, the organist would play the National Anthem
and everyone would stand and sing, before rushing for the
exits and bursting out blinking in the lunchtime sun, ready
to go off and play at being the Lone Ranger or the Cisco Kid.

Left *Two girls play on the fringes of a Gypsy camp in Kent. The traditional wagons were still a familiar site in the Fifties, but they didn't soften attitudes to Gypsies and Travellers, who were regarded with suspicion and hostility by much of mainstream society.*

Right *A boy gives his friend a drink from a beer bottle during a bout of boxing on a bombsite. For working-class lads growing up surrounded by dereliction, boxing was becoming a popular pastime, inspired by American heroes like Rocky Marciano, Floyd Patterson, Sugar Ray Robinson and Jersey Joe Walcott.*

YOUNG WARRIORS *Looking straight out of a scene from William Golding's new novel* Lord of the Flies, *published in 1954, a group of boys indulge in a spot of savage adventure amongst the wilds of Wimbledon Common. A dry day, some open land and a bit of natural cover were all a boy needed for the perfect afternoon of imaginative play.*

A fair wind

• •

With a bit of human assistance, a model sailing boat floats
out from the bank of Victoria Park lake in London. Model
boats were very popular in the Fifties and you could spend
hours down at the local pond, imagining the tiny crew
upon your treasured ship making their way across the
South China Sea. Most boats were either sail powered, like
this one, or clockwork, like the ones the boys are keeping
back. Neither offered any real semblance of control. You
generally put it on the water, waited to see which direction
it decided to go and then ran around to that side of the lake
to await its arrival. More often than not it would run out
of puff mid-stream and you could be waiting for hours, or
else dad would have to wade in and fetch it out. But there
was always some Flash Harry with a remote-controlled
boat, buzzing around showily, coming back to port when
summoned and drawing envious glances from all the other
boys on the lake.

BOYS WILL BE BOYS *A gang of schoolboys take their chances with the cruel sea as a wave crashes into the promenade at Seaford in East Sussex. Going out with your friends, taking your life in your hands, getting soaked… it was all part of everyday life for an energetic young lad in the Fifties.*

Out in the countryside, the old ways were still in force. While hop-pickers gather the harvest at a farm in Kent, their children get their thrills aboard a traditional hay wagon pulled by a shire horse. This was proper wind-in-your-hair travel without the pollution.

Young love blossoms beneath the washing lines strung across a street in Cowcaddens, Glasgow. Scenes like this, with laundry hung out between the slum tenements, would become a fading memory as run-down areas like Cowcaddens came in for extensive regeneration during the Fifties.

Imaginative, resourceful, ingenious, daring: this is how children of the Fifties remember themselves. The excitement of the games they played relied to a greater or lesser degree on the bounds of their imagination. Even a game of football required you to imagine that a pair

Make Your Own Fun

of jumpers were goalposts. As a consequence, there were constant disputes as to the position of the crossbar.

Most residential streets were still the territory of children and for many their only playground. Pavements would be marked out for hopscotch, walls chalked with football goals and cricket stumps, lampposts played the part of trees and the kerb was a place to sit and catch your breath. But as much old housing was replaced with high-rise flats, the sense of community and the street as a meeting place began to disappear. Purpose-built playgrounds were provided, supposedly a safer environment for children yet somehow lacking the soul of the street and the proximity to one's front door. Road traffic became more of a threat and children had to learn a whole new set of rules to protect themselves from the growing dangers of life outside the home.

STREET LIFE *Children enjoy the freedom of a designated 'play street' in London. While cars were allowed for access, it was as if the streets had been designed and built primarily as a stage for children to play upon, acting out their fantasies of war, motor racing, mountaineering or motherhood.*

Girls of various ages gather for a game of hopscotch, a simple but compelling game that girls understood and boys could only wonder at. The layout of the paving stones was perfect for the game's markings and chalk was readily available, being the main writing medium for schoolteachers.

Back in the days when English football was the envy of the world, a bunch of boys honed their skills in time-honoured fashion on the streets of London, trying to emulate Stanley Matthews, Billy Wright or the Busby Babes, whom they sometimes saw in newsreels at the cinema.

DANGEROUS TOYS *A coal truck becomes a new plaything for this group of young lads looking for adventure during the summer holidays. Society was still learning about the dangers of mixing motor vehicles and children and often it was a case of learning the hard way.*

Car trouble

A toy car on a flat road could be a mixed blessing. They looked smart and had all the promise of a high-speed ride of a lifetime, but they were powered by pedals that you pushed back and forth: a laborious process that required enormous effort and offered precious little speed in return. While you pedalled for all you were worth, you scraped your shins on the metal frame of the bodywork. The best bet was to get friends to push you, but then they would run out of steam and the car would slow to a halt within a matter of yards. Then it was your turn to push. The girl in this picture clearly understands the futility of it all.

But the Fifties did see the invention of some classic toys and simplicity was the key. Barbie dolls, Frisbees and Play-Doh all appeared for the first time and toys that had previously been made of metal or wood, like guns, model trains and hula hoops, were now available in plastic.

The archetypal image of a tubby kid tucking into a piece of cake. But few children were overweight in the Fifties, even after sweet rationing ended in 1953. Active lifestyles and simple diets rich in fruit and vegetables meant that obesity was far less prevalent than it is today.

From an early age children were encouraged to get out from under their mothers' feet and play outdoors, not coming back in until they were called in for tea. These three little urchins have brought their toys outside and are settling in for the day.

HANDS UP! *A posse of primary school boys patrols the high street, their weapons a mixture of Second World War sub-machine guns and Wild West rifles and handguns. Despite the recent experience of the war, it was not deemed psychologically damaging for boys to spend their time pretending to kill each other.*

For most children in the Fifties, the first taste of school meant a brick building with high windows and wooden desks with inkwells. In winter they were often cold, draughty places, especially the outside toilets, but boys still wore shorts all year round and girls wore pinafore dresses.

School Days

Children were expected to do what they were told and obey school rules. Parents expected teachers to instil discipline and would invariably take the teacher's side if ever troublesome incidents arose. Children who stepped out of line or failed to do their work could expect some form of corporal punishment, such as the cane or the slipper or a ruler across the knuckles. That didn't mean children were all conformists; they just had to be more ingenious about how they rebelled.

Rebelling was rife when it came to school lunches. Diabolical dishes like tapioca pudding often ended up in school satchels, to be disposed of on the way home. Each child received a third of a pint of milk free every day, which was often semi-frozen in winter or curdled in summer.

AWAY IN A MANGER *A primary school teacher conducts the timeless ritual of the school Nativity play. Christian prayers and Bible stories were standard across the education system in the Fifties, but the Nativity play was more about the music and who would get to play Mary.*

Tutu train

People's roles in society continued to be redefined throughout the Fifties and for girls one of the appropriate pastimes was deemed to be learning ballet. Prompted by magazines like *Girl*, and inspired by the great Margot Fonteyn (aka Margaret Hookham from Reigate in Surrey), girls – mostly from the middle class – were encouraged to attend one of the growing number of local ballet schools, where they would receive a valuable education in deportment, expression, grace and discipline.

But ballet school was not the sole preserve of little girls. Boys often attended too, until they were old enough to notice that they were surrounded by girls in tutus rather than boys with footballs, by which time the teaching they had received in balance and agility had stood them in good stead for their teenage years on the sports field. Ballroom classes were also de rigueur for youths and young adults, with formal dances still playing an important part in the courtship ritual. Even with the arrival of rock'n'roll, the tradition for formal dance endured throughout the Fifties.

COPYCAT *Copying was strictly forbidden and a girl caught doing so might expect a rap from a ruler across her knuckles. Most primary school children wrote in pencil until they were deemed ready to use a nib, which they dipped in ink kept in an inkwell integrated into the desk.*

School dinner is served by a determined-looking dinner lady. It took considerable strength to serve up that mashed potato and even greater mental fortitude to eat it. And just when you thought it was over, pudding would be served, a horror of strange frogspawn-like substances with a blob of jam in the middle.

A sight to set every sweetshop owner's pulse racing: a group of schoolboys press against the glass, waiting for the doors to open so they can fill their pockets with the unrationed bounty inside. Sixpence would buy you a decent assortment, but it had to last the week.

Let's get physical

Physical Education, or 'Games' to give it its more optimistic title, was a ray of light in the otherwise gloomy world of school: a chance to get out of the classroom, a promise of freedom, an antidote to Latin. The aim was to produce perfect physical specimens; the result was a generation of traumatized individuals for whom the sight of any man in a vest and tracksuit bottoms would forever induce panic. For PE teachers were an angry breed. Woe betide the child who couldn't do the crab without giggling.

The kit, like the teachers, was Spartan: no colour, no frills, no elastic. If your shorts didn't fit they fell down – simple as that. You soon learned. But once a term you'd forget about handstands and somersaults and you'd get all the apparatus out and play 'Pirates' – a daredevil game of chase using the full dimensions of the gym. The winner was always the kid who could climb to the top of the rope and stay there; the losers went to hospital. It was the one class everyone looked forward to.

MILKING IT *Pupils help themselves to their daily ration of a third of a pint of milk. This was made available to all students under the age of 18 by the 1944 Education Act, but somehow it never quite tasted how milk should and few children relished the arrival of their mid-morning drink.*

Not all kids were happy with their lot in the Fifties. Children who didn't fit into the mould, or didn't get on with their peers, could be left feeling very isolated and misunderstood. Eventually these suppressed emotions would find their expression in the counter-culture of the late Fifties and Sixties.

A new school in a new town. The opening of comprehensive schools, like this one in Hemel Hempstead, ushered in a new era for the secondary education system, mixing boys and girls and children from all backgrounds in a Utopian vision of equal opportunity for all.

The family unit was of great importance and everybody was expected to play their part in helping it to function. Although more and more women were going out to work, the majority of households consisted of a father who was

Meet The Family

the bread-winner, a mother who was the housewife and children who did what they were told. Children who transgressed would be chided with the threat, 'Wait 'til your father gets home.' Corporal punishment such as smacking was generally accepted as the best means of instilling discipline. 'Spare the rod and spoil the child' was the motto.

But children didn't live in permanent fear of their parents. Dinnertime was spent together at the table, chatting about the issues of the day, listening to the wisdom of father and the gentle instructions of mother. 'Elbows off the table!' 'Don't talk with your mouth full!' And afterwards children helped to wash up and clear away.

In short, children were expected to replicate their parents' lives and lifestyles, but this notion would soon be called into question.

LUNCH BREAK *A little boy watches as two girls walk off to work in the Hull fisheries, following in the footsteps of their mothers. Most people lived near their work and walked home at lunchtime to eat before returning for the afternoon shift.*

Left *Two little boys watch and learn as their mother shakes out the mat. It was a time when children learnt the art of keeping home at their mother's side, always maintaining a safe enough distance to avoid being hit by a backhander for getting in the way.*

Right *With women going to work in increasing numbers, often it became the work of the older children to take care of the little ones. It wasn't always ideal. If big brother fancied a kick-about with his friends, baby might find herself playing the role of goalpost for a couple of hours.*

TEA TIME *Meal times were family times and that meant sitting down at a table all together and talking. It was how the family really got to know each other and learned what everyone was up to. This family are enjoying a boating holiday on the Norfolk Broads.*

Holiday fun

Summer holidays were the highlight of the year for families in the Fifties. It was a time when fathers could relax, and forget about the demands of work as well as the time constraints of commuting. Once he had closed the front door and was out of earshot of the telephone in the hall, he was beyond reach. Work couldn't call him up on a whim to ask if he'd seen the stapler, or send him a pile of documents to read through by the morning. He could switch off completely and spend some quality time with his children, albeit still wearing the full jacket and tie like this chap on Bournemouth beach. There were still standards to maintain!

Mum relaxed on holiday too. She could wear her new summer dress and walk barefoot on the sand. And sharing the workload of looking after the children was a welcome relief after all those months of housewifery. The net result was a sense of lightness and jollity within the family and a feeling that special treats were always around the corner, like an ice cream or a donkey ride or maybe a trip to the fair.

Nearly there!

After running half the length of Britain's longest pier in Southend, a little girl finally makes it into the arms of her waiting dad. Southend was a popular destination for weekend excursions from London, along with Margate, Eastbourne and Brighton. Families that were fortunate enough to own a car would take it out for a spin on a Sunday, maybe for a picnic among the green fields or to their nearest seaside resort. Dad would drive, mum would sit beside him watching the scenery go by and the children would sit in the back saying, 'Are we nearly there yet?'

But already the grim experience of the bank holiday traffic jam was becoming a familiar feature of British life and the recently nationalized British Rail did its best to encourage people to make their excursions by train. Advertisements for seaside resorts like Blackpool, Brighton, Skegness and Butlin's holiday camps carried the slogan, 'It's quicker by rail', and for most people, rail or coach was still the best option for getting out of town.

SUNDAY BEST *It was traditional to dress up smart for social occasions on Sundays, though perhaps not quite as flamboyantly as this extended family of Pearly Kings and Queens from London's East End. Each London borough had its own Pearly family who helped to raise money for good causes.*

Crowning moment

1953 saw the most historic event of the Fifties take place, the coronation of Queen Elizabeth II, coinciding with the second most historic, the conquering of Everest by Edmund Hillary and Tenzing Norgay. The British were not new to coronations; this was the fourth of the century (and it also turned out to be the last); but this time the whole event would be captured on television and broadcast to the nation. For the first time in history, the British people could all join in the pageant, provided they knew someone with a television set and a living room large enough to accommodate the entire street. More than 20 million people did just that, nearly half of the population tuning in to the pioneering BBC coverage.

The convenience of television didn't stop people coming out in droves to see the procession in the flesh. This mother and son were typical of the crowds that lined the route from Westminster Abbey to Buckingham Palace, sleeping out overnight in order to assure their place on the big day.

A favourite pastime of little girls was to play mummies and daddies and create their own families with dolls, cuddly toys and even pets. This was their interpretation of the idyllic family life, in which babies were easily pacified and dogs were always glad to do balancing tricks.

A mother and son on the doorstep of their family home. Working mothers were growing in number but, unaided by the state, they were having to find their own way of juggling their working lives with the pressures and responsibilities of being a mother and wife, which they were still expected to fulfil.

FAMILY PHOTO *Three generations of the Smith family of Lambeth are captured on film for posterity. Here was the archetypal British family: matriarch and patriarch, three offspring, all married with a child of their own. The extended family was a powerhouse and Sundays were often spent socializing together.*

Left *A girl from a family of West Indian immigrants reclines on her luggage at Victoria Station, waiting to see where life will take her next. Life was tough for the immigrants of the Fifties and the family unit was often their best protection against racial prejudice and poor living standards.*

Right *A boy walks on a wall, supported by his mother. You can imagine his sense of achievement. There's nothing like feeling so tall and adventurous (but safe at the same time).*

HOLIDAY HOME *Caravanning became popular in the Fifties as people in need of cheap accommodation sought alternatives to the traditional bed & breakfasts run by fearsome landladies. They allowed you to keep your family together under one roof, albeit tinny and cramped and lacking in the essential facilities that we would later come to expect.*

Neighbourhood watch

In some parts of Britain, the concept of family extended beyond your own front door and embraced the whole neighbourhood. Indeed, families often lived in the same street, and so family and community were one and the same. It was commonplace to leave your front door open so that neighbours could come and go, effectively turning the street into one big communal hall off which each family had its own space.

When you had finished the housework and had nothing to do, you could just stand in your front doorway and watch the world go by, keeping an eye on the comings and goings of the folk around you, who were taking an equally keen interest in everything that went on. It was social, familiar and public spirited, but it did mean that it was very difficult to keep any secrets. During the Fifties a lot of these neighbourhoods were demolished, being deemed too crowded and cramped. The residents were mostly rehoused in high-rise flats, destroying at a stroke the communal forum that they had enjoyed on the street.

Bridging the gap
· ·

Days out with dad would usually have some educational element to them. On Saturday afternoons he might take you to the football so that you could become indoctrinated in the worship of your local team, just as he had and his father before him. If your team were playing away, you'd have to find some other form of entertainment to while away the afternoon until it was time to huddle round the wireless and listen to the scores being read out. So dad would take you to see something interesting, or at least something that he thought was interesting, like a bridge or a tunnel or a chimney. 'Look at the craftsmanship in that!' he might exclaim, as you gazed on nonplussed. You would then be regaled with the history of said artefact, together with a few salient bits of trivia, which would wash over you like water off a duck's back until one day, long into the future, you would find yourself with children of your own, trotting out exactly the same fascinating facts to an uncannily similar reception.

Days We Remember

We don't remember the wet summers. We remember the sunshine glinting off the waves, the breeze blowing off the sea billowing mum's floral dress and playing havoc with her hair. We remember grandad with his trouser legs rolled up, the chill of the salt water lapping over our feet and making ripples in the sand. We don't remember the drab days stuck indoors with nothing to do; we remember trips to the zoo or the museum, marvelling at the giant animals, live or stuffed, and dreaming of being an African explorer or an archaeologist digging up dinosaur bones.

We remember street parties for the coronation, where everybody came out to play and cheer and sing, and we remember the seasons: snow in winter, sunshine in summer, daffodils in spring, conkers in autumn. Everything looks clearly defined in hindsight; even the pea-souper fogs that choked London hold a nostalgic significance, representative as they are of a time when we were young and innocent and happiness came from the simple pleasures we made for ourselves.

Above *Putting up the bunting as the East End of London prepares to celebrate the coronation with a good old Cockney knees-up. Steps were scrubbed, white surfaces whitewashed, balloons blown up and streams of bunting strung out across the street and between houses. There was no doubt that this was a significant moment in British history.*

Right *A hat that's too small and a tie that's too big: the essential accoutrements of a good street party. The whole of the country came out of their houses to celebrate the Queen's coronation in a collective show of patriotic pride – once they'd finished watching it on TV, that is.*

HOWDAH PARTNERS
Children visiting the zoo could not only see the elephants, they could ride them too, like these visitors to London Zoo. It was a thrilling and occasionally alarming experience and accidents did occur from time to time, resulting in the practice being stopped in the early Sixties.

Left *A day at the races. Pigeon racing became hugely popular among working-class men in the Fifties, particularly in the north of England. Once referred to as 'the poor man's racehorse', a good pigeon would often receive more attention, affection and indeed conversation from its owner than his own wife and children.*

Right *A boy gazes spellbound at one of a family of stuffed giraffes on display at London's Natural History Museum, while his father nurtures his interest with a constant stream of noteworthy facts about the beasts. Following an experience like this, a boy could hold forth about giraffes to his friends for weeks on end.*

FUNNY FACE *A children's entertainer practises the ancient art of gurning during a laughing competition on the Isle of Wight. They understood the value of a funny face in the Fifties and weren't afraid to pull one if the situation required it. It meant instant laughter guaranteed.*

Seafood diet

A visit to the seaside meant seafood. Wherever you went around the country, you could expect to find 'the best fish and chips in Britain', all for a couple of shillings (about 10p in today's money). For the Cockneys of east London who took the sea air at Southend in Essex, the specialities were cockles, whelks, winkles and, most esoteric of all, jellied eels. Like rhyming slang, jellied eels were designed to distinguish the Cockneys from the rest – the rest being the people who turned green at the mere sight of them. But Cockneys lapped them up, literally, often with an accompaniment of pie and mash and liberally sprinkled with vinegar and pepper. Consequently, seaside towns in summer would give off an intoxicating mixture of aromas: the salty ozone of the sea itself, mingled with the tang of vinegar and the whiff of boiled or fried fish. The scent would follow you all the way home in the carriage of the train or the seats of the coach. And like all smells, it would distil into a memory, of sunshine and sand and endless amusements.

Autumn meant conkers and conkers meant conker fights. All sorts of methods were employed in an attempt to turn the humble horse chestnut into a steel-hard weapon of war. Baking and soaking in vinegar were common, but ultimately it was the speed of your hand and sharpness of your eye that mattered.

Market day in Kingston-upon-Thames and, apart from the two schoolboys, the traditional fish stall is attracting a distinctly older clientele. Most big towns still had their markets but an increasing amount of custom was being directed away into the new, supposedly more convenient supermarkets.

Get your skates on

This picture captures two great passions of the Fifties: pram racing and roller skating. In a decade when more and more people were discovering the thrill of private motoring, there was a general gravitation towards anything with wheels. Races involving prams, wheelbarrows and go-carts became regular features of holiday celebrations. Whole villages would turn out to watch races, which often involved refuelling stops at the pub and always threw up hilarious thrills and spills.

Roller-skating, though, was an altogether more serious obsession. Street skating was popular but the big draw was the skating rink. The rink had a big, wooden floor, dusted with chalk for grip, and you'd stay there for hours, everybody skating round and round in the same direction, then, on a given signal, all skating the other way. Anyone who tried to cut across would be reprimanded and sometimes made to sit out. The noise of the wooden wheels on the wooden floor was deafening. At the end they'd play the National Anthem, you'd hand in your skates, collect your coat and leave.

ROARING 'EM ON *The Millwall FC mascot, a lion, provides the razzmatazz at an FA Cup match against Birmingham City. It was more than enough in those days; the crowd created the atmosphere, packed into vast terraces, singing and roaring in unison and each man hoping that they, and the men behind them, could avoid the call of nature for 90 minutes.*

Left *A father takes his chances in a latter-day re-enactment of the William Tell legend, a cigarette in the mouth taking the place of an apple on the head. He appears to be oblivious to the likelihood of becoming yet another casualty in one of the new NHS hospitals, having the arrow and rubber suction cup prised off his forehead.*

Right *The Fifties brought a breakthrough in the development of a vaccine against polio, a disease that had reached epidemic proportions since the war. By the end of the decade, it was virtually eradicated in Britain, thanks to a programme of immunization. These children are bravely awaiting the first of two injections.*

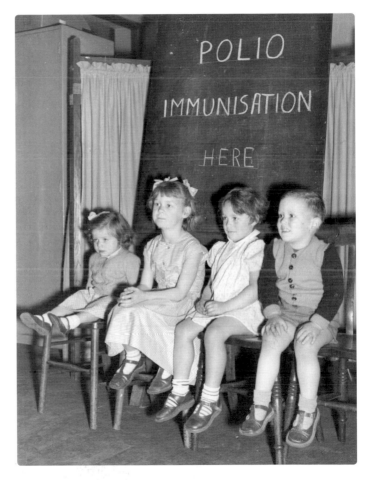

LET'S ROLL! *Every child wanted to learn to roller-skate and here we have a perfect demonstration of the right and wrong way to do so. The boy in the middle has it right, leaning forward, his arms in a controlled swing to establish momentum. The boy to the left has got it wrong.*

Breakdown

• •

The British car industry responded to the growing demand for private cars with a flamboyant array of stylish motors and practical family cars. Legendary models like the Morris Minor, Ford Anglia and Vauxhall Victor led the world in car design and were becoming the essential luxury items of the age. By the end of the decade there were about five million cars on the road – one for every fifth household – and rising rapidly.

With car ownership and the freedom of the open road came car trouble and the misery of the roadside repair. A good day out could be spoiled by the alarming rattle of some vital engine component working loose, the disheartening rumble of a flat tyre or the sight of steam billowing out from somewhere beneath the bonnet. Almost overnight, fathers had to become pit lane mechanics, adept at operating manual jacks, changing wheels and poking parts of the engine while inhaling sharply through their teeth. Garages and breakdown services did a roaring trade. Mothers, meanwhile, had to become even more patient.

GIDDY UP! *In the holidays, everyone made a beeline for the seaside resorts like Blackpool, where you could find an enchanting array of entertainments and wonders. Saddled up on a donkey, you could imagine yourself as the Lone Ranger with Tonto by your side, just as you'd seen at the pictures.*

Two dancing girls take time out to model the latest fashions on the seafront at Blackpool. New synthetic textiles were giving designers the freedom to really experiment, but the polka dot cotton dress, with a high waistline and billowing skirt, was a Fifties classic.

The new, more expressive approach to fashion meant a wider variety of cuts, colours and patterns and the freedom to accessorize your outfit with an impromptu hat if you so desired. These spectators at the Wimbledon Tennis Championships set a lasting trend by unselfconsciously wearing a newspaper to keep the sun off.

Teenagers in love

By the end of the decade, the young generation had found its voice. No longer mini models of their parents, young people were developing their own culture and their own way of life. Swing and jazz were on the wane; the new music coming from America was rock'n'roll, loud and lively and full of attitude and angst – emotions familiar to adolescent kids but threatening and alienating for their parents. A generation gap was opening.

The icon of the new youth culture was the Teddy Boy. Taking their style from the clothes of the Edwardian era (hence 'Teddy'), Teddy Boys and Teddy Girls were distinctive in their dress and hairstyles and demonized by the media for their loutish behaviour. Violence amongst teenagers became a growing concern for society and the term 'juvenile delinquent' was coined. In reflecting this trend, cinema also served to fuel it, with films like *Blackboard Jungle* and *Rebel Without A Cause* offering a new, thought-provoking view of society. There was no stopping it. The 'teenager' had been born and was here to stay.

Left *While the Fifties saw a number of electrical appliances coming into use, such as vacuum cleaners and washing machines, there were still certain jobs that required good old-fashioned elbow grease. Scrubbing the steps may have burned off calories, but it also played havoc with your knees.*

Above *1956 saw the passing of the Clean Air Act, a series of measures designed to make smogs like this a thing of the past. A combination of smoke and fog caused by pollution from domestic fireplaces and power stations, smogs were a familiar feature in London, culminating in the Great Smog of 1952.*

HOME FROM HOME *By the end of the decade the British were beginning to discover commercial air travel to holiday destinations abroad, but the vast majority still sought their summer fun at home. Holiday camps, like this one at Butlin's Filey, were hugely popular, providing families with all the communal activity, comfort, fun and affordability they desired.*

By the end of the decade the smoke was lifting and Britain was steaming forward into a bright new future that promised less toil, more leisure, better entertainment and broader horizons. 'They've never had it so good,' was Prime Minister Harold Macmillan's assessment, but everything was about to get a whole lot better.